Freaky Facts about Spiders

MINNETONKA, MINNESOTA

Two-Can Publishing
11571 K-Tel Drive
Minnetonka, MN 55343
www.two-canpublishing.com

Written by Christine Morley
Illustrated by Phillip Morrison
Edited by Nadia Higgins
Cover design and Mac production by Joe Fahey

Many thanks to Debbie Folkerts, professor of biology at Auburn University, Alabama, for lending
her considerable expertise on spiders.

Photographs:
p. 4: © dscott/David Meharey/iStockphoto.com; p. 5: Bruce Coleman Inc; p. 6/7: CLAUDE
NURIDSANY & MARIE PERENNOU/SPL/Photo Researchers; p. 8/9: © Hans Christoph
Kappel/naturepl.com; p. 10: DAVID SCHARF/SPL/Photo Researchers; p. 11: © Tim Gainey/Alamy;
p. 12: REG MORRISON/AUSCAPE/Minden Pictures; p. 14/15: Oxford Scientific Films; p. 16/17: ©
JAMES CARMICHAEL JR./NHPA/Photoshot; p. 18/19: Rod Preston-Mafham/Premaphotos Wildlife;
p. 20: CLAUDE NURIDSANY & MARIE PERENNOU/SPL/Photo Researchers; p. 21: Bruce Coleman
Inc; p. 22: © Ken Preston-Mafham/Premaphotos Wildlife; p. 24: © Ken Preston-
Mafham/Premaphotos Wildlife; p. 25: © Brian Kenney/Oxford Scientific Films; p. 26/27:
UNIVERSAL/THE KOBAL COLLECTION; p. 27: MARVEL/SONY PICTURES/THE KOBAL
COLLECTION; p. 28: DANIEL HEUCLIN/NHPA/Photoshot; p. 29: © Ken Preston-
Mafham/Premaphotos Wildlife; p. 30: © MITSUHIKO IMAMORI/Minden Pictures; p. 31 (top): ©
DANIEL HEUCLIN/NHPA/Photoshot; p. 31 (bottom): Image # AMNH-FL-19032A/AMNH
Department of Invertebrate Paleontology

Library of Congress Cataloging-in-Publication Data
Morley, Christine.
Freaky facts about spiders / [written by Christine Morley ; illustrated by Phillip Morrison].
p. cm.—(Freaky facts)
Summary: "Introduces a variety of arachnids and the amazing ways they live, hunt, breed, and
defend themselves"—Provided by publisher.
Includes index.
ISBN-13: 978-1-58728-596-7 (hardcover)
ISBN-13: 978-1-58728-597-4 (softcover)
1. Spiders—Miscellanea—Juvenile literature. I. Morley, Christine. Totally amazing spiders.
II. Morrison, Phillip, ill. III. Title.
QL458.4.M65 2007
595.4'4–dc22
2006022589

Printed in Singapore

1 2 3 4 5 11 10 09 08 07

What's Inside

Spider Basics

Do spiders creep you out? Well, don't worry! Most of them are much happier munching on insects than nibbling on you. So get ready—you are about to enter the totally freaky world of spiders!

Spider Breakdown

A spider's body is made up of two sections—a cephalothorax and an abdomen. The cephalothorax includes the eyes and two razor-sharp fangs. Eight spindly legs also belong to this section. The abdomen holds organs such as spinnerets for spinning amazing spider silk.

A SPIDER FLAT ON ITS BACK

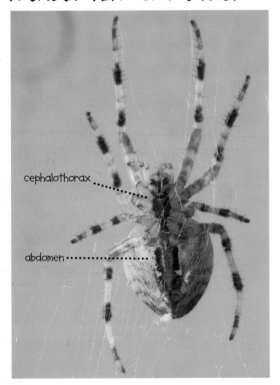

cephalothorax

abdomen

What's in a Name?

Spiders belong to a bunch of animals called arachnids. Arachne was the name of a girl in an ancient Greek story. She beat the goddess Athena at a weaving contest, so Athena changed her into a spider.

Just my luck!

Where in the World?

Spiders live everywhere on Earth, except Antarctica. They make their homes under rocks and logs, in tunnels and trees, and also underwater. Spiders have been rocketed into space to see if they still spin webs without gravity. They do!

▲ A tiny crab spider may spend days, or even weeks, on the same flower petal. It holds out its long front legs, ready to ambush a passing insect.

HA HA! What's a spider's favorite day of the week? Fly-day. HEE HEE!

Home Sweet Home

Spiders build incredible homes, from cozy burrows to underwater bubble houses. Many spiders rig their homes with traps and trip wires to capture prey.

Staying Cool

How does a hairy tarantula avoid the sizzling desert heat? It digs a deep bunker in the sand. The underground den keeps the spider nicely chilled until the sun goes down and the air turns cooler. Only then will it creep outside to find a bite to eat or a mate for the evening.

Hey, chill out.

It's a Trap

The spider in the photo has rigged up trigger threads around its nest. If an insect disturbs them, the spider feels the threads move. It knows a tasty meal is nearby.

▲ Bugs beware! A spider's nest can also be a trap.

That's Weird

Cave spiders are excellent at rock climbing. They have extra-strong, long legs to help them grip and climb up the steep walls of their caves.

Spider Cities

Social spiders work together in construction teams to build enormous spider cities. These spiders connect huge sheets of webs, making one giant web big enough to cover a tree. Social spiders also feed in groups so that they can catch and share larger prey.

Life in a Bubble

A water spider builds its home underwater. It weaves a silk platform. Then it traps an air bubble from the surface and attaches it to the platform. When the air begins to run out, the spider pops up to the surface for another bubble.

Through the Trapdoor

The secretive trapdoor spider lives in a tunnel with a tightly fitting door. When visitors approach, it opens the door and eats them!

▲ A trapdoor spider's burrow is expertly constructed. The spider makes sure that its home is coated with soil. Then it adds soft layers of spit and silk.

Waiting Game

A trapdoor spider spends many evenings at home, waiting patiently below its door, sometimes with its front legs just sticking out. When the spider feels the vibrations of passing prey, it rushes out, grabs and bites the prey, and drags it into the burrow. Then the spider firmly bangs the door shut.

That's Weird

One kind of trapdoor spider plugs its burrow with its hard, flat rear end. Its abdomen fits tightly into the hole, like a cork in a bottle. Now the spider is safe from enemies.

Come on in!

9

Super Spinners

Spider silk is tough, light, and elastic. It's perfect for making a comfortable bed, a dangerous trap, a lasso for prey, or a rope swing to escape from danger.

Look, I'm Tarzan!

Spinning Silk

Spiders spin different kinds of silk for different jobs. When the spider first spins the silk, it is liquid, but it soon hardens into thread that can be stronger than steel.

SILK FOR KEEPING EGGS SAFE

SILK FOR DRAGLINES

SILK FOR WEBS

SILK FOR WRAPPING PREY

What a Drag

A spider can always make a getaway. Wherever a spider roams, it leaves a trail of thin silk thread, called a dragline, which works just like a rope swing. When the spider is threatened, it jumps on to the dragline and swings to safety.

Under the Microscope

This picture has been magnified many times. It shows silk being spun from tiny tubes on the spider's body.

Sticky Habit

Why doesn't a spider get caught in its own web? A web is not sticky all over, so a spider avoids the sticky threads. It also coats its body with slippery oil so that the silk doesn't stick.

Strange but True

A spider eats about 2,000 insects a year. Without spiders, the world would be overrun with bugs.

▲ A spider wraps up its prey to keep it from escaping.

Web Masters

About half of all spider species spin webs for catching insects. Webs come in all kinds of shapes and sizes, including ones that look like big string bags, bicycle wheels, and hammocks.

A Deadly Net

A net-throwing spider doesn't sit on its web like other spiders, but holds the web in its four outstretched front legs. When an unsuspecting insect walks by, the spider stretches the net out wide and drops it over the victim's body. The web is stretchy enough to wrap up a big moth.

▲ A net-throwing spider's huge front eyes allow it to spot prey in the dark.

ORB SPIDER'S WEB

An orb spider spins a silk bridge between two twigs...

> Whee!

...then swings down to add supporting threads.

It spins threads from the middle to the edge, in the shape of bicycle spokes on a big wheel.

> Over and under, in and out, and back again.

Then, the spider spins from the middle outward. It goes round and round.

> This part always makes me dizzy!

Finally, it spirals back to the middle of the web. This time, it lays a sticky thread to catch its dinner.

Super Strong Webs

Every night, most orb spiders spin a bouncy web. The web contains so much thread it could make a pair of silk tights. The threads are light enough to blow in a breeze but extremely strong. The silk must be strong enough to hold the spider, which is 4,000 times heavier than its web.

That's Weird

A spider's web is packed with healthy nutrients. Before a spider spins a new web, it makes a nice big meal out of the old one!

> Mmm, web again... delicious!

Horrible Hammocks

The hammock weaver spider has a sneaky plan. It spins a flat or slightly domed net of silk. Above the net, it sets up a mass of tangled lines to knock flying insects onto the net, or hammock, below. The spider just waits in its hammock for a tasty insect to fly along and land in its bed!

On the Prowl

Many spiders are fierce warriors. They go out on patrol, ready to hunt down and attack creatures that wander into their paths. Others leap on their victims, glue them to the spot with sticky spit, or even worse...

Surprise Attack

The jumping spider has huge eyes that detect even tiny movements of passing insects. First, it creeps up on its prey. Then it jumps, opening its jaws mid-flight to deliver a lethal bite when it lands on its victim.

Strange but True

Some jumping spiders can leap as far as 40 times their body length.

▲ A jumping spider is a champion long jumper. It crouches down like a cat, pushes with its back legs, then leaps forward.

What's in a Name?

The spitting spider is named after its gross habit of spraying prey with two streams of gruesome goo. This goo causes the prey to fall to the ground. The spider has plenty of time to stroll over and kill it.

SPIDERS ARE GOOD AT SPORTS

On your mark...

A wolf spider is a large and hairy athlete. It can look for prey in four directions at once. When it sees something, it sprints after it with deadly speed.

Expert Thieves

A few kinds of spiders steal food from other spiders' webs. The burglar spider moves quietly and unseen over another spider's web, nibbling up old scraps of food. When it is really brave, it eats the main prey, too.

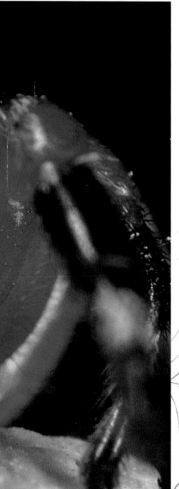

Soon you'll be mine!

The fishing spider spends its days dangling its front legs in ponds. The legs can sense ripples made by a struggling insect that has fallen in. The spider grabs the unlucky creature and reels in its supper.

Fangs and Food

Spiders are experts in the art of poisoning. A spider releases venom through fangs that look like curved claws beneath its eyes.

Works every time!

Portia Spider

The Portia spider is a real cannibal. It creeps into another spider's web and tugs on the silk. The web owner crawls toward the intruder, thinking it has trapped an insect. Then the Portia spider attacks, kills, and eats the surprised web spider.

DINNERTIME!

A spider stuns or kills an insect with venom from its needle-sharp fangs.

fangs

Then, it spits a cocktail of juices onto the insect to turn it to pulp.

Finally, the spider sucks the insides out of the insect, leaving just its hard, crunchy casing.

These black fangs are small but powerful. The venom that shoots ough a spider's fangs can be far more poisonous than snake venom.

Fussy Eaters

A banana spider's favorite food isn't bananas. It's the cockroaches that live on bananas. Banana spiders eat little else, so people use them to help control the cockroach population.

Some spiders refuse to feast on anything but wood lice. The fussy spiders pierce the wood louse's tough casing with their enormously long fangs. Now they can get at the juicy body inside.

The Deadly Few

Though most spiders are poisonous, most spider bites won't harm you. There are only a few nasty biters that are dangerous to people.

▲ The female black widow spider is about the size of an adult's thumbnail and is highly poisonous.

Black Widows

The black widow spider likes to keep to itself. It will bite only when it feels its life is threatened. The spider bites people because it often lives in people's shoes and clothes. One small bite is enough to make a person very sick and can sometimes kill.

Danger Down Under

The Australian funnel web spider wanders around backyards in search of dinner. If it is disturbed, it will attack and deliver a harmful bite that's strong enough to pierce your fingernail. Victims may even die!

That's Weird

The deadly violin spider has marks on its body that make it look like a violin. Usually its bite isn't fatal, but the wound can take a long time to heal and leave a large scar.

On the Defensive

Spiders are always on the lookout for prey, but predators are also on the lookout for spiders. Clever disguises and quick getaways help keep spiders out of trouble.

Tiny Spears

The hairs on some spiders are sharp with hooked ends. Many big, hairy spiders shoot clouds of hairs into the faces of predators. The hairs cause so much irritation that the spider has plenty of time to run away.

Rotten Disguise

Some spiders avoid dangerous predators by disguising themselves as bird droppings. One kind of bird-dropping spider even spins specks of white silk around itself on a leaf. This makes it look like a fresh dropping.

Spot me if you can!

Good Disguise

Many spiders keep safe by looking exactly like leaves. These spiders are mottled to match bark or moldy leaves, green to match living leaves, or even have brown, jagged outlines to look like dead leaves!

HA HA! Why did the spider steal a car? To take it for a spin. HEE HEE!

Alien Bug

If you were a hungry predator, would you eat something that looked like a spaceship? The buffalo spider has a flat body, spiky spines, and bright colors. Predators are so confused by the spider, they walk away in search of an easier meal.

Strange but True

A spider from Madagascar disguises itself by resting on a twig. It looks just like a dried-up bud.

That's Weird

A South American tree-dwelling spider leaves its enemies all wet. It simply raises its rear end toward its attacker and squirts liquid in its face.

A Date with Danger

When courting, the first thing a male spider does is to persuade the female spider not to eat him!

HA HA! What did the spider couple send in the mail? A webbing invitation. HEE HEE!

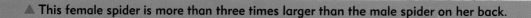
▲ This female spider is more than three times larger than the male spider on her back.

That's Weird

A few male and female spiders are friendly. One will tug on the web to let the other one know it wants to meet. Then they tap their legs together as if they were playing "patty-cake."

Perfect Present

One type of wolf spider knows that the way to reach a female spider's heart is through her stomach. He presents his mate with a gift of a wrapped fly. While the female munches her meal, the male mates with her. He knows that as long as she is busy eating her present, she won't eat him!

I think she likes me!

Message of Love

Many kinds of male spiders wave their long, hairy legs at female spiders as a sign. It shows they want to get to know them, not be eaten for dinner! Some of these dance routines can be quite complicated, with all kinds of tricky steps—especially when performed with eight legs!

WATER SPIDERS GET TO KNOW EACH OTHER

One kind of water spider announces he's on his way to a female by sending drum beats across the water. Then he pulls on her dragline and tows himself across the water to meet her. They strike up a romantic conversation by tapping each other's legs.

A kind of fishing spider finds an area of a pond where a female spider has set up house. The male finds the female by following the fragrant scent she has left on the water.

How It All Began

Some female spiders take great care of their eggs, wrapping them in a bubble of silk called an egg sac.

▲ A female nursery-web spider takes care of her egg sac. Many other spiders abandon their eggs.

Spiderlings

Eggs hatch into spiderlings. Some, such as burrowing spiderlings, are completely cared for by their mothers. But lots of other spiderlings have to fend for themselves. When food is short and they are hungry, they may even eat each other!

Wheee!

Some spiders take to the skies, especially young spiderlings that travel long distances to find homes of their own. They glide on loose strands of silk that catch the breeze, rising to heights of 5,000 feet (1,525 m). This is called "ballooning."

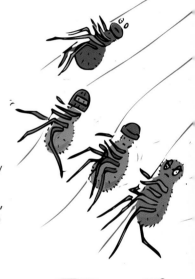

A REAL SIDE-SPLITTER

Every time a spider gets too big for its skin, it just grows a new one.

Ooops—I'm splitting up!

First, a split appears across the spider's back. The split grows and grows.

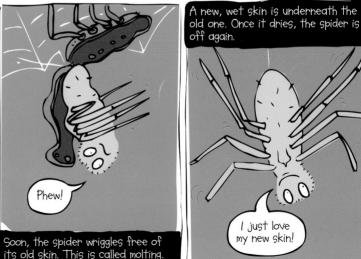

Phew!

Soon, the spider wriggles free of its old skin. This is called molting.

A new, wet skin is underneath the old one. Once it dries, the spider is off again.

I just love my new skin!

Spider Stories

Around the world, there are hundreds of stories about spiders. They feature everything from hairy, scary monster spiders to half-human spiders with super powers.

MONSTER SPIDER...CRAWLING TERROR 100 FEE

TARANTU

Imagine being attacked by towering tarantulas! Killer spiders were the gruesome inspiration behind this movie from the 1950s.

Spider-Man

A spider has special grip pads on its feet that allow it to walk up walls and across ceilings. This amazing ability was the inspiration behind the cartoon character Spider-Man. He can "weave a web as strong as steel" to catch his enemies, too.

RESEARCHERS SEEKING CLUE!

CAN ANYTHING ESCAPE IT?

He'll never find me here.

Ceiling Thomas

In West Africa, the rascally hero of many stories is half-man, half-spider. He's called Anansi. When things are going his way, Anansi is a man. When he's in trouble, he turns into a spider and hides on the ceiling—a habit that's earned him the nickname Ceiling Thomas.

That's Weird

"Little Miss Muffet" was a real person from the 1600s. Her father was a spider expert who insisted she eat mashed spiders. Until 200 years ago, this was thought to be a cure for the common cold.

Spiders and People

Chances are, dozens of spiders are crawling around your home this very second. Is that a good thing or a bad thing? Here are more amazing facts to help you decide...

It's a Setup!

Most spiders, like this wolf spider, are harmless, but they're often blamed for other bugs' bites. The real culprits are usually blood-thirsty ticks or fleas that are too small to see. The bugs quickly depart, leaving a nearby spider to be blamed for a crime it didn't commit.

Wonder Webs

Spider webs could help to save people's lives. The U.S. Defense Department is attempting to use stretchy spider silk to make bullet-proof vests. The steel-like threads are strong enough to absorb the power of a flying bullet. Wow!

A Helping Home

In New Guinea, there are giant wood spiders that spin webs 6 feet (2 m) wide. The huge, sticky traps are so sturdy, the people who live there use them as fishing nets!

Holy Spiders

Some people believe spiders have special powers. In the South Pacific, it's said that you reach heaven by climbing a giant ladder of spider silk that stretches up into the sky.

Spiders Save the World

Would you like to share your home with this leggy visitor? A house spider, like most spiders, is harmless and does a great job of killing flies and other insects that spread disease. Each year, spiders eat thousands of tons of dangerous bugs. Yuck! In fact, spider venom is so powerful at killing bugs that some people would like to bottle the stuff and sell it. The venom could be made into a safe and natural bug spray.

29

Spider Hall of Fame

There are more than 35,000 kinds of spiders crawling around the planet. Have a look at some of the record-breakers among them.

The Itsiest-Bitsiest

You'd need a magnifying glass to get a loo at the smallest spider in the world. The record goes to the mygalomorph spider of Borneo, an island country in Southeast Asi This spider's entire body would fit on the head of a pin.

Mean Machine

A Brazilian wandering spider must be the meanest spider on Earth. It hides away in people's homes, and it won't think twice about giving a fatal bite. You can't even scare it away. If you hit the fearless fiend, it will try even harder to bite!

Old Grannies

Most spiders live for about a year, but some of the bigger ones live quite a bit longer. Male tarantulas can live eight years or more, but the prize for the longest-living goes to the females. Some female tarantulas and trapdoor spiders can live 20 years or more.

Hairy and Humungous

Who's the biggest of them all? The Goliath birdeater tarantula. This creature's hairy legs can span 10 inches (25 cm)—about the size of a dinner plate. But don't judge a spider by its size. Though this tarantula can eat prey as big as mice, it is nowhere near as deadly as some of its smaller relatives. It spends most of its time burrowing in soil in South America's rainforests.

Ancient Legs

When it comes to old, dinosaurs have nothing on spiders. The oldest spider fossils show that spiders were crawling around 380 million years ago. That's more than 150 million years before the first dinosaur showed up.

Fast and Famous

Imagine cheetahs with eight legs. For their size, they still wouldn't be as fast as spiders. And the award for the fastest of the fast goes to the giant house spider, who's really only about half an inch (16 mm) long. This guy races along at just over 1 mile (1½ km) per hour. For such a small creature, that speed is enough to land the giant house spider (known also as *Tegenaria gigantea*) in the *Guiness Book of World Records*.

Tricky Words

abdomen (AB-duh-muhn): the back end of a spider, which contains its spinnerets

arachnid (uh-RAK-nihd): a member of a group of insect-like animals that includes spiders, scorpions, and ticks

burrow: a hole or tunnel under the ground where some spiders live

cephalothorax (SEF-uh-loh-THOR-aks): the region of a spider's body that includes its eyes, mouthparts, and legs

dragline: a strand of silk that a spider trails behind its body

egg sac: a furry pouch in which a female spider lays her eggs

fang: a sharp, hollow mouthpart that a spider uses to inject venom into its prey

spiderling: a baby spider

spinneret: the part of a spider that produces silk

venom: the poisonous liquid that a spider injects into prey with its fangs

Index

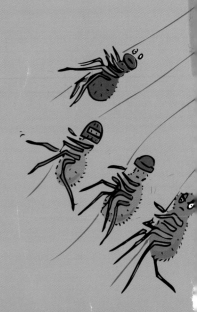